Mirabelle's Forest Garden

Written by
Ina Curic

Illustrated by
Kelemen Kinga

Bucharest, 2017

To all the visionaries who put their head, heart and hands together in the service of creating more harmony with and on the Earth!

Published by Imagine Creatively
www.imaginecreatively.com
Design by Mariel Cernat
Edited by Jill McKellan

Copyright © 2017 Ina Curic
All rights reserved. No part of this book may be used or reproduced in any manner without the express written permission from the author and publisher.

Mirabelle's Forest Garden/ Ina Curic;
illustrated by Kelemen Kinga
ISBN-13: 978-973-0-25797-7
ISBN-10: 9730257973

A CIP record for this publication can be obtained upon request from Romanian National Library.

[1. Gardening for children - Fiction. 2.Garden Design -NonFiction]
I. Kelemen, Kinga, illustrator II. Title

Summary: A little girl is walking through her village collecting seeds, support and advice for a forest garden project in her community.

"All the world's problems can be solved in a garden."
Geoff Lawton

Dear Reader,

Mirabelle invites you to enter a special gardening game where you can plan, play, observe and experiment with a sustainable gardening ethic.

A forest garden or food forest is based on the woodland eco-system incorporating different layers of vegetation that are working together, being mutually supportive. The result is a way of working the earth that is diverse, productive and sustainable ecologically.

Any garden can incorporate principles and techniques from forest gardening with fast beneficial effects for biodiversity, soil fertility and food production.

The story book includes:

- Reflection questions throughout to keep the interest of smaller children and engage with the story. You can also leave the story to stand on its own and return to the questions on later readings.
- An interactive section at the end with further info about plants and other story elements.
- A glossary explaining terms included in the book.
- References to initiatives that connect children and forest gardens.
- Answers to the reflection questions included throughout the story.

The story seeks to inspire children, families and schools to learn about and experiment with sustainable gardening. We can grow our own food as a community that takes care of the earth and all of its beings.

One garden at a time!

Ina

Mirabelle was a little girl who loved plants, gardening, and all things outdoors. It did not matter if it was windy or rainy, sunny or snowy. She always had fun outside.

But there was one thing Mirabelle loved best. This was gardens. She loved to look at all the food and flowers in them. They smelled wonderful too. To put a garden and a forest together is something she'd like to do.

One day Mirabelle decided to make a dream garden of her very own. It would be pretty and special and many plants and trees would grow. She sat down under the large tree in her backyard and began to think of what she would need.

There was much to do.

Mirabelle decided to visit her great grandmother. She was wise and always had a table full of good food. Surely she could help.

When Mirabelle got to Granny's she smiled warmly. "Come in, my dear. I have something good for you if you can help me in the garden."

Mirabelle's eyes lit up.

"Is it something sweet, Granny? I am hungry for some of your good food too. Can I have some cauliflower popcorn or my favourite pickles first? I'll gladly help you with the garden too."

Mirabelle and Granny then walked to the garden.

Self heal: one of granny's favourite plants.

•Question 1:

Can you recognize some of the plants and vegetables granny has in the attic?

•Invitation:

Find grandmothers in your community that hold old knowledge of plant uses and benefits. Ask them about their favourite plants!

Granny,
I need help for a special garden theme.
A forest garden is part of my dream.
Full of tasty food in beautiful colours
And smells to show all the tasty flavours.
I want perennial plants,
which come out every year.
also shrubs, fruit and nut trees.

Granny shook her head and wrinkled her nose.
"I don't know how to make a garden like that, my dear, but I am sure you'll find a way to make it grow. You can take seeds from my garden and some of the herbs to get you started."

Mirabelle continues her visit to her uncle next door who was very skilled with trees.
She wants to speak with him too about her dream.

•**Question 2:** Do you know plants that can help your body when you have a cold or a cough?

•**Invitation:** Try drinking plant infusions when you have a cold, noticing the different flavours. Learn to identify medicinal plants in natural environments.

At first her uncle was confused.

"A forest-garden? Hmmm ... This is not possible. It is either a forest or a garden, not both together. You should find another dream."

But Mirabelle knew she had the right dream:

"My dream will come true, you will see.
It will be a garden that has more than one tree.
It will be earth that is magical in more ways than one,
Gifting us with clean food grown with water and sun."

"Can you help me have trees where many fruits will fit? I imagine apples and cherries of red and yellow together. Our land is not big but growing up to the sky is free."

Mirabelle smiled and clapped her hands when uncle said he agreed. He would teach her how to grow varied fruits on one lovely tree. They would take branches from all her favourite coloured cherries and grow them into one. By the time they were grafted his work would be done.

When Mirabelle asked how they did that her uncle said:

"My dear, you see, trees befriend branches from similar trees."

"What happens next?" She asked with widened eyes.

"They will grow and fuse together to become your own unique tree," her uncle replied.

She knew that would be a very special tree.

Now it was time for Mirabelle to visit her grandpa who lived in the woods. He was a skilled craftsman and some of his advice would do her good. Grandpa knew all about trees and which ones would work best so she could have a dream garden unlike the rest. Mirabelle began to explain her dream:

"What I see is a forest and
a garden and so much more.
It's also a wild playground
and a school that nature can store.
We can relax and laugh and even sleep,
In a hanging hammock close to a creek."

"Grandpa, can you help to build some playgrounds in my special forest-garden-to-be? I want a tree house and platform so I can watch deer coming out of the forest."

The way Grandpa looked at Mirabelle was hard to understand:

"Be reasonable, my darling. A forest garden? I just don't think there is any such thing."

Mirabelle pleaded again: "This garden is going to be so special, with fruit trees and flowers and delicious veggies. Please help to make my dream come true".

Grandpa clapped his hands and said, "OK. I'm in!"

Mirabelle was excited about her grandpa agreeing to help. She continued on her way to share what she wanted to do with everyone else. And slowly it all became clear. The time to begin her dream garden was drawing near.

•**Question 3:** Can you see things an animal, bird or insect would like to eat in this picture?

"A place to walk, rest, play, and work.
And learn about nature as an extra perk.
Filled with many butterflies and bugs,
Wild pheasants, baby hares to play with and hug.
All creatures would be welcomed with a big heart,
Because each of their presences would play a part.

Everyone sharing in nature's bounty,
Maybe even from county to county.
This garden will be a place to pick food
Or eat dinner in a tree that tastes good.
Wouldn't this be neat?
Who wouldn't love such a treat?

Forests and gardens are also schools,
Teaching children nature's rules.
Kids would love this, I am so sure.
Who wouldn't stay at a place
So lovely and pure?"

By the time Mirabelle arrived to visit her aunt she was incredibly excited. The forest garden wasn't just going to be good, it was going to be amazing.

Her aunt lived by the forest where she often went to pick mushrooms. She didn't understand why would Mirabelle want to work so hard on such a thing. Mirabelle answered with a sing:

"To help the bees and the flowers and all the plants grow, while also showing how nature loves all."

Mirabelle pointed to her aunt's mushroom basket, smiling: "You can grow your favourite mushrooms in the forest garden with fruits and flowers into the bargain."

Her aunt agreed to help her learn all about mushrooms and which ones to pick. Because that is important so one doesn't get sick.

"You can also grow your own mushrooms on logs in the shade", the aunt added. "Or hang some mushrooms from trees. When conditions are right, their spores can spread and you can have a great harvest to pick".

Mirabelle was very eager to start her garden. Her auntie had agreed to teach her so many things.

- **Question 4:** How many mushrooms can you count on the forest floor and on the logs?

- **Question 5:** What role do mushrooms play in the forest as fungi?

There was one last family friend that Mirabelle wanted to visit. What she learnt there would be important to consider.

"Flowers of many colours I want to see.
They will bring beneficial insects and many a bee.
They will work together as a community should,
And help the flowers grow and smell so good.
Also, the harmful bugs will stay away,
And make the garden better every day.
Maybe even the right birds will come to play,
And they will all want to stay."

Mirabelle's friend said that she could give her many roses to use. They are edible, beautiful and smell delicious too. They add splashes of colour that attract lots of lovely insects. Since Mirabelle was a little girl, maybe she'd give pink roses too. To which Mirabelle replied, "That's great, I prefer rosemary though." The two laughed at her joke.

*"Good guardians for any garden
Are the lady bugs and the spiders.
Then marigolds of all sorts
And many other medicinal herbs.
Not one is alone, we know,
They fare much better in
good company."*

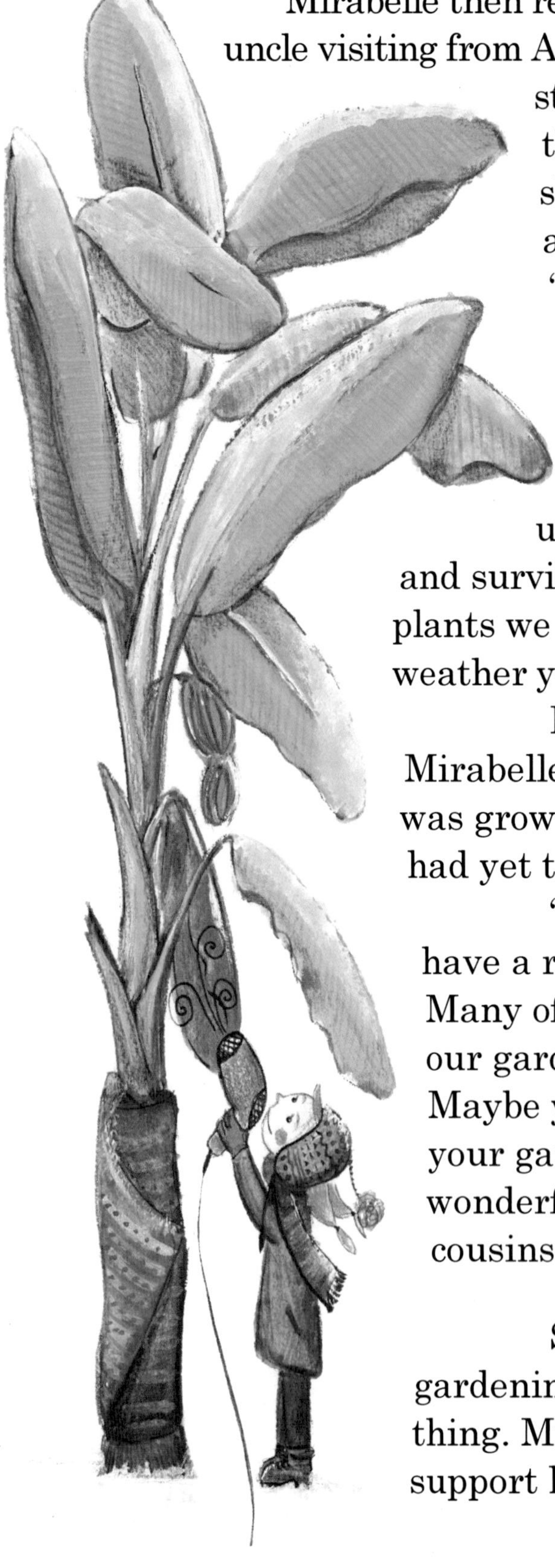

Mirabelle then returned home to meet her cousins and uncle visiting from Africa. They were filled with smiles and stories to share. Uncle got Mirabelle thinking about what plants from Africa she could grow. The bananas were very appealing.

"How do you grow them?" she asked.

"For banana plants you need a tall glass house here. You could add another level to the greenhouse you have that is partially underground. Bananas cannot get cold and survive you see. There are many other plants we grow that can't handle the freezing weather you have."

His words were very smart and Mirabelle learned a lot. This forest garden was growing bigger and sprouting, and she had yet to start.

"As for us, her uncle added, we don't have a really cold winter down south. Many of your plants would live happily in our garden throughout the year. Maybe you can share seeds some day, when your garden is made. We can start a similar wonderful garden with your cousins back home".

Sharing seeds and joy over gardening even across continents was a great thing. Mirabelle felt wonderful to have others support her dream.

Her friend Khalil came along and he sat down by her to talk. They began to write notes, draw sketches and work out a plan to create it.

Seven magic layers of forest garden were needed to come to the fore.They would start by planting fruit and nut trees that would grow to be a tall canopy. Then they'd plant dwarf fruit trees, and below shrubs and bushes with colourful fruits for birds and children alike. There'd be herbs then ground level plants like strawberries, and others that would climb up the other plants to reach for the sun.

Finally Mirabelle remembered her aunt: "We'd better not forget what's going on under the ground. What plants or mushrooms can we grow that help look after the soil?"

Together, all these different plants would form a garden unlike any that most people have seen. It would be a forest and a garden in one magical scene. A happy family of nature and people in harmony for all to see and believe.

Then Khalil said something that made Mirabelle's heart bloom: "My family also has some land, I think they'd love a forest garden like we've planned."

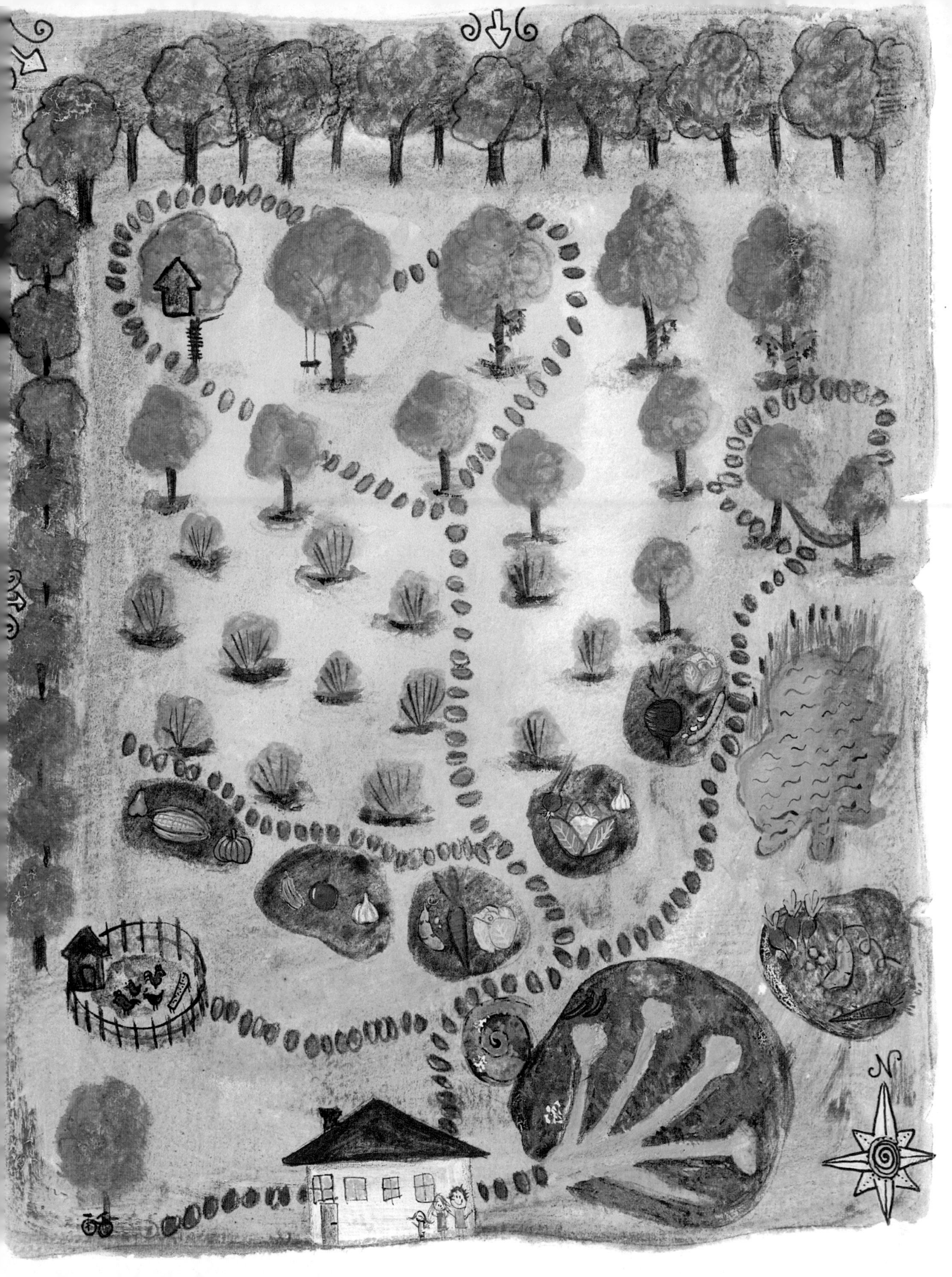
N

Mirabelle realised that her dream was going to come true. She knew there was much more to learn and she would have to ask for help. But at least she was off to a good start.

It was an idea from her heart for a community of family, friends, plants, trees, animals, insects and really - all living beings! A beautiful garden for all to share.

Mirabelle counted everyone she met that day as part of her support community.

They all saw the wonder of her plan.

A forest garden was good for the environment, just as much as it was good for people. It would produce more than food: smiles and happiness too. Also a great home for many of the earth's creatures that would live in harmony with a big family of plants and trees.

It would surely take a while because some plants grow very slowly. By the time she was done with her school years, which she'd only just begun, there'd be a fruit and nut mountain to harvest, eat and share!

Mirabelle shared a few last words that she wanted everyone to remember:

"A place for everyone, kids and adults alike.
We can all play in here and eat with delight.
Experiment if you want to watch something grow.
Until you try, you will never know."

•Invitation. Consider plants you would put in your ideal garden. What would you love to harvest and eat?

Wonder about Mirabelle's dream journey?

What are perennial plants?

Unlike plants that live for one or two years, perennial plants come out of a strong root and multiply for many years. Many of the annual plants that have been improved in time, like spinach, have wild perennial relatives or alternatives. What is exciting about perennial plants is that they can help your garden expand over the years without extra work!

Jerusalem Artichoke (Helianthus Tuberosus)
is an excellent perennial potato alternative.
It withstands winter temperatures down to -30 Celsius (-22 Fahrenheit) and produces year after year, with great health benefits both raw and cooked.

Multiple purpose plants

Mirabelle searches for plants that can serve multiple purposes in smaller, more confined gardens. Many wild and cultivated plants have multiple qualities and roles:

-Edible and very nutritious;

-Herbal medicine, use in teas or as first aid (e.g. for stings or cuts);

-Attractive for bees and other beneficial insects that eat garden pests;

-Protective of other plants through strong odours or attractive colours.

Plantain (Plantago Officinalis)

This plant has edible leaves, flowers, and seeds. It is used to help heal cuts and wounds and it also reduces inflammation caused by insect bites. When outdoors, plantain is always handy as first aid. Crush a leaf and put it on the sore spot, trusting its magic!

Pot Marigold (Calendula Officinalis)

This is a medicinal plant that is very healing for external and internal wounds. A tea or gargle made of calendula helps with healing sore gums or throat. The leaves and flowers are both edible and bring joy to every salad or dessert. The roots and leaves have strong odours that protect other garden plants from various insect and worm pests.

Underground green house

Mirabelle's parents already have an underground greenhouse which could be raised one level.

Underground greenhouses are dug into the earth in order to use the earth's constant temperature. They require less additional heat in winter. The original design for such a greenhouse comes from Bolivia and was called a walipini, an Aymara Indian word that means "a warm place." This is a simple and relatively cheap type of greenhouse that allows food production all year long even in climates with very cold winters.

Beneficial spiders

Spiders - who are arachnids not insects - play a special role in any garden. These little creatures are amazing companions who eat many pests that affect garden plants, in some cases even more than the birds eat. You can watch spiders weaving webs or eating their prey.

Did you see how the dew turns their webs into crystal castles early in the morning?

Pay attention to different types of webs spiders weave depending on the environment.

Cauliflower Popcorn?

You can try one of Mirabelle's favourite dishes: a raw recipe for popcorn made from cauliflower.

You only need four ingredients. Combine together raw cauliflower (cut in small pieces to resemble popcorn), nutritional yeast mixed with any cold pressed oil and a pinch of salt.

Simple and delicious. Especially when you grow your own cauliflower!

Eat mirabelles!

Did you know that mirabelle is a type of plum also known as the mirabelle prune (Prunus domestica subsp. Syriaca)?

Mirabelle plums are popular in Europe and Asia where they grow both wild and cultivated. Year after year, the trees yield a great harvest of red, yellow and orange fruits spread out from May-June to September-October in temperate climates.

The wild varieties grow fast from seed, are disease and frost resistant and can be used as an edible windbreak.

Glossary

Beneficial insects

Beneficial insects/bugs are any species of insects that perform valued services like pollination and pest control.

Companion planting

The close planting of different plants that enhance each other's growth or protect each other from pests.

Graft

A shoot or twig from a mother plant inserted into a slit on the trunk or stem of another living plant, from which it receives sap and to which it gives the characteristics of the mother plant.

Forest garden

Designed eco-system that combines agriculture and forestry. It includes different layers of mutually supportive vegetation from large canopy, fruit and nut trees to shrubs, vines, perennial vegetables, and herbs.

Forest school

An educational approach that offers learners regular opportunities to achieve and develop confidence and self-esteem through hands-on learning experiences in a woodland or natural environment with trees.

Mycelium

The vegetative part of a fungus, consisting of a network of fine white filaments (hyphae). Mycelia move through soil or other environments, like logs or straw, and can then create fruiting bodies, commonly known as mushrooms.

Perennial plants

Plants that live and give yield several years in a row, having a persistent root from which a new plant develops every spring.

Permaculture

Permaculture refers to the development of agricultural ecosystems intended to be sustainable and self-sufficient. It is also called simply "permanent agriculture". Forest garden is a feature included in standard permaculture designs.

Questions answered

1. Plants hanging to dry in Granny's attic from left to right: lavender, dill, red hot chilli peppers, red onions, mint. Dill is part of Umbelliferae family with flower heads similar to carrot, celery, parsley.

2. Many plants and spices, commonly used in kitchens, can strengthen the body to deal with colds: echinacea, yarrow, garlic, onion, ginger, cloves. Plant infusions that ease coughing include: wild thyme, linden, mint, oregano, chamomille.

3. A squirrel would gather and eat nuts. A cow or goat would graze grass. Deer chew and rub against the bark of young trees. Berries in the bushes are an attraction for birds. Flowers are a food source for nectar feedings insects such as bees, butterflies or mosquitoes.

4. Mushrooms on forest floor: eight. Mushrooms on the logs: thirty seven.

5. Mushrooms are the fleshy fruiting body of a fungus. Fungi have an important role of cycling energy in the eco-system. They can break down tough organic materials like those in fallen leaves and dead trees, making them available for easier digestion for other forest creatures. Some species of fungi form beneficial relationships with plant roots, helping to transfer nutrients through the soil.

Further References

Food Forest Card Game www.FoodForestCardGame.com
Children in Permaculture www.childreninpermaculture.com
Outdoor Classrooms www.outdoorclassrooms.com.au
The Permaculture Student www.thepermaculturestudent.com
Institute of Permaculture Education for Children
www.permaculture.us.com

Did you enjoy this storybook?

Please share the story in your community &
leave a review here on www.amazon.com
to help others discover it!

Imagine Gardening Creatively

Joining Mirabelle in pursuing earth-friendly dreams?

Get free posters to inspire your gardening adventures:
www.imaginecreatively.com

Stay tuned for the forthcoming
Mirabelle's Gardening Guide
to further inspire you to start or
upgrade your sustainable gardening!

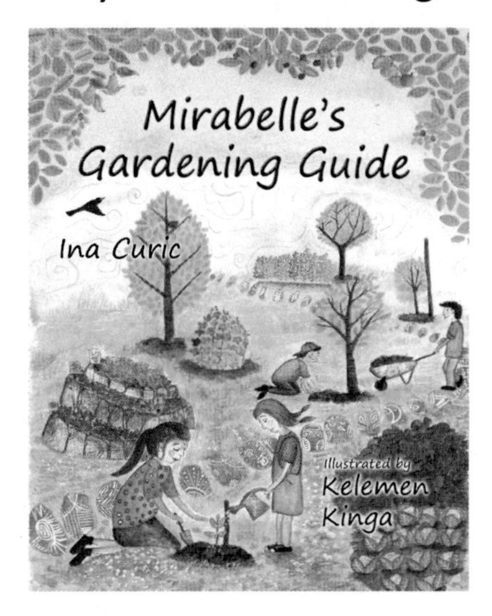

Other titles by Ina Curic

Anagrania's Challenge

Try creative conflict resolution with a princess that has the courage to express herself in thiscoming-of-age story!

A Golden Grain Princess endures many imposed and stressful fashion trials that leave her determined to rise up against the impositions and find a creative solution.

A message about whole grain nutrition as well as accepting and celebrating one's uniqueness.

Queen Rain, King Wind - *The Practice of Heart Gardening*

Family harmony secrets are not told. They are practised.

A story about heart gardening. Learn how to water the seeds of joy in any relationship.
Two elves visit Queen Rain and King Wind. They convince them to disperse the clouds and dry the tears in their relationship that are falling continuously and endangering the life of bees on Earth.

Guidance and practical examples are included for family practice of appreciation rituals.

Rainbow Bridge - *The Ho'oponopono Magic*

A story about the four most important words to repair any relationship. It seems too simple. But it is.
Two elves are traveling to the Castle of Sun and Moon to retrieve the light and colours that had been missing on Earth, endangering the harvest. Finding the Sun and the Moon upset with each other, the elves gift them a magic formula called ho'oponopono to restore their relationship backto harmony.

Check out free gifts at the author's website:
www.imaginecreatively.com

Made in the USA
Las Vegas, NV
28 July 2021

27156595R00021